You Know You're Irish When ...

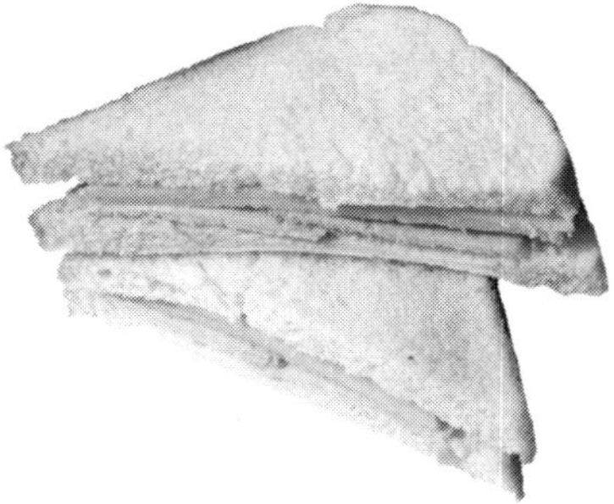

Seamus Ó Conaill

THE O'BRIEN PRESS
DUBLIN

First published 2015 by The O'Brien Press Ltd.,
12 Terenure Road East, Rathgar, Dublin 6, Ireland.
Tel: +353 1 4923333; Fax: +353 1 4922777
E-mail: books@obrien.ie
Website: www.obrien.ie
ISBN: 978-184717-778-0

Internal illustration by Emma Byrne.

10 9 8 7 6 5 4 3 2 1
19 18 17 16 15

Layout and design: The O'Brien Press Ltd.

Printed and bound Printed and bound in the Czech Republic by Finidr Ltd.

The paper in this book is produced using pulp from managed forests.

... 90% of your sick days are on Mondays. The other 10% are Tuesdays after bank holidays

... it's not a fizzy drink. It's a 'mineral'

... your house has an unused 'good room' that is three degrees colder than the rest of the house

... the back door to your home is the front door

... you understand the biggest division in Irish society is between Lyons and Barry's

... you're proud we're all poets and writers, but feck it, who's read Joyce?

... you've been to a funeral
of someone whose name
you didn't know

... 'tis awful he's dead ... now where are the 'hang sangwiches'?

... it takes you three days
to recover from Halloween

... you have to get a dispensation from Rome to turn on the immersion

... in college, one third
of your dinners were
breakfast rolls from Centra

... another third of your college dinners were hot chicken baguettes from Centra

... and the final third of
your college dinners were
curries at 2am

... you've used the phrases, 'Go on, Go on, Go on, Go on,' and 'They *all* have lovely bottoms,' in the last year

... you won't give the Brits
a point in the Eurovision,
but fair play to them, they
gave us eight

... you'd never admit it, but you're secretly proud that we've won the Eurovision more times than anyone else

... you never go to Mass, but you'll get the baby christened. How else will little Oisín get into a good school?

... you're twenty-five and you bring your washing home to Mammy

... you're thirty-five and you still raid Mammy's fridge

... you thank the bus driver

... you clap when the plane
lands

... you hate Ryanair, forgetting the hundreds you paid for flights in the 1980s

... you ask taxi drivers if they're having a busy night

... when going on holiday, you pack Barry's Tea, Tayto crisps and Denny sausages

... You know the *real* meaning of the word 'shift'

... you ignore celebrities
– 'Who the hell does your
man think he is?'

… Mammy let you watch all the violence and swearing on TV you liked. But God forbid there was any 'sexy' stuff going on

... your first kiss was at the Gaeltacht

... you groaned when Mammy joined Facebook, but accepted her anyway. Now she's plaguing your friends

... your young fella is a genius compared to the muppets in fifth class

... you appreciate what makes a good crisp sandwich: Dairygold butter, Taytos, and Pat the Baker sliced pan

... you only ever used one strap of your schoolbag, nearly giving yourself scoliosis, because you were 'in with the lads'

... you did nineteen hours of homework a night for the Leaving. And the teacher still thought you were shite

... you'd throw yourself in the river before you'd listen to a foreign actor do an Irish accent

... you’d pawn your Granny for an All-Ireland GAA ticket

... you ignore the matches all year. But you'll be drinking pints and singing in the streets when the county team wins the All-Ireland

... you've pretended to laugh when your English mates asked you to say 'Thirty-three and a third' when really you wanted to kick them in the balls

... you once paid seven Euro for a pint in Temple Bar and have never set foot there since

... you say 'yes' to every invite, certain that you mean it the odd time

... most of your childhood breakfasts were either Weetabix or Cornflakes. And your feckin' cousins had Frosties

... you have a love/hate relationship with TK Lemonade

... you met your wife outside a pub. You were the slick operator with the white and green lighter from Centra

... you know that road signs are merely an indication of distance and direction

... you only know one verse of the Rosary and the National Anthem. The rest you mutter and mime

... after you turn forty, you find yourself buying the local paper for 'the deaths'

... you complain about how shite the Rose of Tralee is, but you always watch it

... you complain about how shite the Eurovision is. Then get angry when all the countries vote for their neighbours

... most of your overdraft in your thirties was spent attending friends' country weddings

... you have an inability to
'pop in' to a friend's house.
All visits take a minimum of
two hours and three boils
of the kettle

... you've still thirty-two years on a mortgage for a house fifty miles away from a town

... Ass? Here, it's arse

... it wasn't the five Sambuccas, the six pints, or the four glasses of wine at dinner. It was the dodgy curry chip

... you’ve never seen the Book of Kells in Trinity College

… the only time you were in a museum was during that school trip to Dublin back in '92

... someone in your class wore a patch to correct a weak eye

… you’ve blessed yourself passing a graveyard, an ambulance, a holy well – even a nun on a good day

... sex education in school was taught by a nun or a Christian Brother

... you can talk and listen at the same time

... you know what swearwords you can get away with around Mammy, the Gardaí, and the priest

... every dinner you ate as a child was boiled

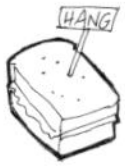

... your Mammy has a pressure cooker that hasn't been used since the 1980s

... you know what 'I'm running five minutes late' really means

... they're not 'errands'.
They're 'the messages'

... you can never get off the phone. Goodbyes to Nana take longer than the rest of the call combined

... you know what is meant by the question, 'Who's she having it for?'

... after fifteen years learning Irish, you can say one sentence fluently: *'An bhfuil cead agam dul amach go dtí an leithreas, más é do thoil é'*

... saying *'Póg Mo Thóin'*
on holidays around
foreigners is great craic

... UHT Milk from 'the continent' sets you off on a rant

... calling someone 'chicken' is a term of endearment

... your father let you change the gears in the car when you were twelve years old

... your holiday tan develops as follows: white, red, blister, peel, white

... all crisps are called 'Taytos', no matter what the brand

... your school closed for the week of The National Ploughing Championships

... you complain about the heat after three days of sixteen degree sunshine

... you say 'sorry' as a response to just about everything

... they'll always be 'penny sweets' no matter how long you're using Euros

... 'Not bad' means that
you're in flying form

... you've had an entire morning ruined after getting stuck behind a tractor

... you organise a house party for when the pubs are closed on Good Friday

... it's St Stephen's Day, not Boxing Day

... all skin maladies in your childhood could be cured with Sudocrem

... you could put a down-payment on a house with the money you got for your Confirmation

... your mam took the phone off the hook to watch the soaps

... you've actually completed the twelve pubs of Christmas

... the annual television highlight of your childhood was *The Late Late Toy Show*

… you’ve been told to stop ‘acting the maggot’

... you caused mayhem in Australia the year after finishing college

... you always hoped for the ring in the Halloween brack, but you always ended up with the cloth

... you got a great kick out of telling your English cousins you got three months off for the summer holidays

... you didn't wear a seatbelt for most of your childhood; it was more a case of hoping for the best

... you never answer the front door without looking out the window in case it's the TV license man

... it’s a week into Lent and you’re back eating chocolate

... as a teen you pretended to go to late mass on Saturday, so as not to have to go with Mammy on Sunday morning

... outside your own county, your accent is incomprehensible

… you vote for your local representative because, sure, didn't your father vote for his father?

... you've no idea what the Irish Seanad does

… you know more about US politics than what's going on in the Dáil

... you've no idea what is the difference between Fianna Fáil and Fine Gael

... you won't leave the
house if so much as a light
dusting of snow falls

... you kept the top
button on your school
shirt undone at all times
because you were 'cool'

... until you were twenty-five, your favourite cheese was EasiSingles

... you've inherited a piece of Waterford Crystal that you don't like, but couldn't possibly throw out

... a finger of fudge is just
enough

... occasionally you sit on the couch and eat a packet of Taytos and a Dairymilk, alternating mouthfuls

... you eat your Christmas sweets in the following order: Roses, Quality Street, Lemons

… you know what 'Mikado' are

... your grandparents used to give you Emerald Caramels as a child. You didn't like the chocolate, but the toffee inside was delicious

... you miss Nana and
her endless packets of
Silvermints

... at least one member of your family eats tomato ketchup with absolutely everything

... you've a rake of fillings from drinking concentrated orange juice in the 1990s

... you broke your collarbone playing with the local GAA team

... your friend broke her nose after getting a smack from a hurley

... your Mammy tore strips off the teacher for giving you a 'C' in Irish

... you still have an Italia '90 T-shirt that you wear to bed on cold nights

... any time a Garda calls to the house, guilt takes hold, even if he's just asking for directions

... you swallowed chewing gum as a child and wondered if it really took seven years to go through your system

… you know saying ‘that’s gas’ has nothing to do with cars or ovens

... on the bus, you put your bag on the seat beside you and look out the window when people hop on

... the bus arrives late
(again!)

... you've a friend who is a writer, but haven't a notion about what they've written

... you've never had a
proper conversation with
your father

... you know where you were when Anne Doyle announced she was retiring from RTÉ News

... your grandparents had
a portrait of the Kennedys
on the wall next to the
Sacred Heart

... you've a very definite opinion about Bono

... you can't see a red
setter without thinking
about the 1960s yellow bus
that took you to school

... you're twenty-four and Mammy worries that you'll never find a 'nice girl', or 'nice boy'

... you expect all roads to be 60% potholes

... you've witnessed a tractor outside Mass on a Sunday

... you were warned as a child you'd get 'square eyes' from looking at the telly

… when you were ‘acting the maggot’ as a child, you were warned ‘wait ‘til your father gets home’

... you've never figured out
how to shut your mouth
and eat your dinner

... you spent part of your childhood worrying that the wind would change and your face would stay that way

... you never figured out
how to wipe that smile off
your face

... you may well have been 'born in a barn', as you've never got round to closing doors

... you do the four claps to
'The Wild Rover'

... people assume you pregnant or on antibiotics because you ordered a Coke at the bar

... you know what a 'farmer's tan' is

... you can pronounce but can't spell 'Taoiseach' or 'Oireachtas'

... at weddings you assume Irish dancing is something innate to you and all Irish people, not something you need to be taught

... 30% of your skin is freckles

... no trip to the doctor
is complete without a
prescription for antibiotics

... you can't wait for the other fella to shut up so you can start talking

... you know an invitation
for a party for half eight,
actually means half nine,
possibly ten

... you'll sing, regardless of whether you know the words

... your heart skips a beat at the sight of clothes that have actually dried on an outside line

... you can finish this rhyme: 'Knock, knock, open wide, see what's on the other side. Knock knock, anymore? Come with me through the ...'*

*magic door!

... you have brown hair, but
a red beard

... school holidays were spent getting shooed outside by Mammy when all you wanted to do was watch Zig & Zag on *The Den*

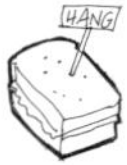

... you're still afraid of the wooden spoon

... you ask someone: 'Are you goin' out, or are you goin' *out* out'

... a good funeral is better than a bad wedding

... you've lit a candle for
someone or had a candle
lit for you

... you’ve more than twenty cousins

... you were warned of all manner of ailments that came from sitting on radiators

... going to bed with wet hair (according to Mammy) is essentially risking your life

... you understand bus timetables are more aspirational than accurate

So How Irish Are You?

Agree with 30+ points : Pfft. Do you even know what a 'Lovely Girl' is?

Agree with 70+ points: A touch of green, but the colour do be as wayke as warter.

Agree with 100+ points: Make up your mind, young fella. A couple more Guinness should do it.

Agree with 120+ points: Now that's the ticket!

Agree with 140+ points: Congratulations, you're the love-child of leprechauns.